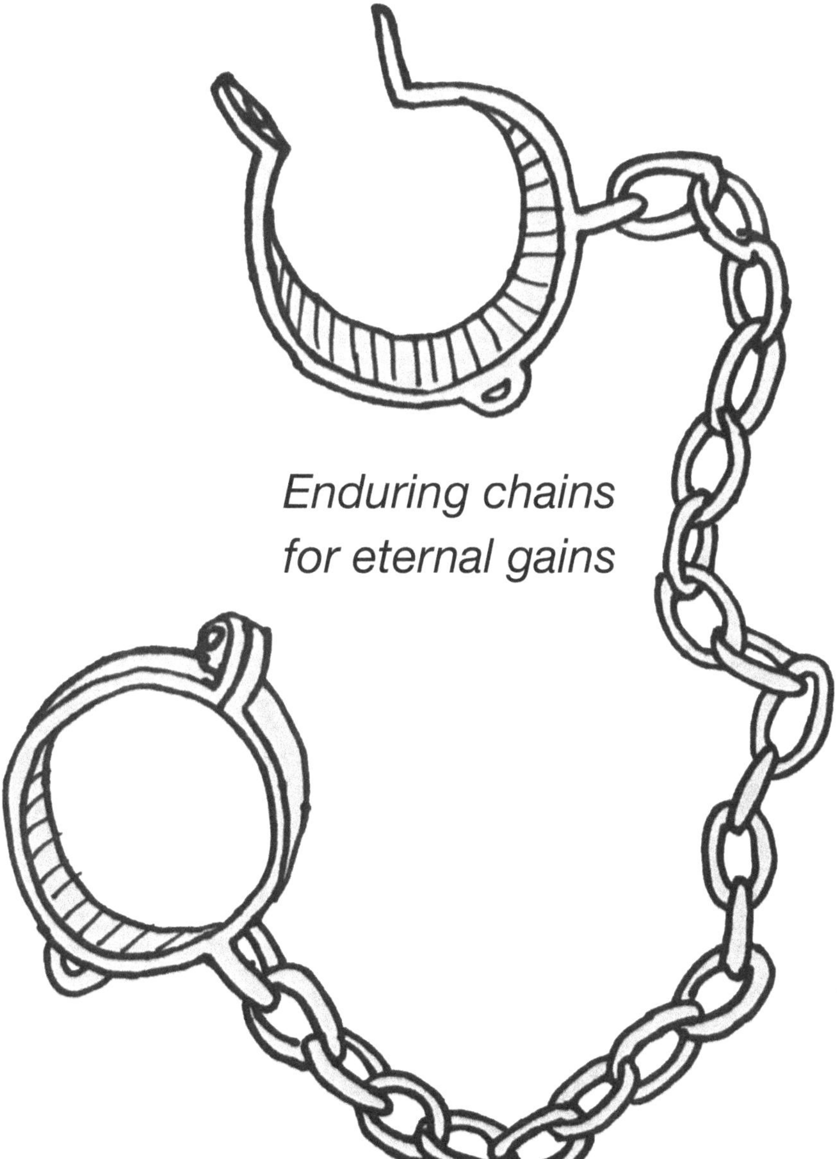

*Enduring chains
for eternal gains*

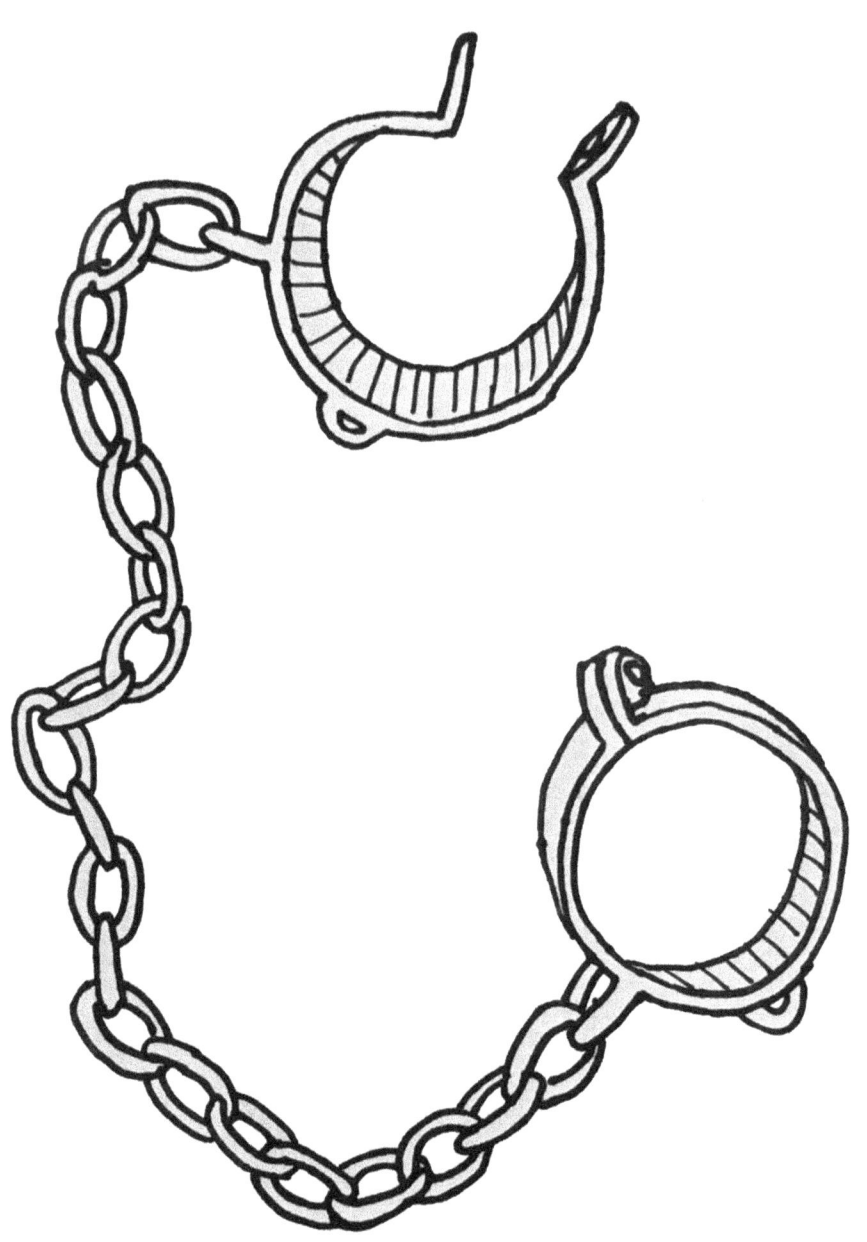

The Little Bird Bible

Philippians

Retweeted

Jarrod Branson Conyers

Copyrighted Material

Little Bird Bible Philippians Retweeted
© 2021 by Little Bird Bible LLC
All Rights Reserved.

No part of this publication may be reproduced, stored in a retrieval system or transmitted, in any form or by any means electronic, mechanical, photocopying, recording or otherwise- without prior written permission from the publisher, except for the inclusion of brief quotations in a review. All images are also under the same copyright limitations.

All characters real, historic, or imagined may have no knowledge or concept of the Little Bird Bible
and thus do not endorse it.

For information about this title or to order other books and/or electronic media, contact the publisher:

ISBN: 978-1-7335122-6-8

Second Edition

Printed in the United States of America
Cover and Interior design: Little Bird Bible LLC.

Dedication:
To the next 500 years of Reformation;
May there be less martyrs,
greater compassion,
and more grace.

Philippians Retweeted	vii
Foreword	vii
What Is Little Bird Bible?	vii
What Makes The Little Bird Bible Different?	vii
E-Reader Sticker Bonus	x
Try Little Bird Bible Abridged	x
Other Key Features	xi
The Backstory of Philippians	1
The Author	1
The Book	1
The Audience	1
Key Places	2
Chapter 1	3
Chapter Breakdown	3
Chapter 1 Emoji Lexicon	4
Chapter 1 & Comment Threads	6
Chapter 1 Reflection & Discussion	12
Chapter 2	15
Chapter Breakdown	15
Chapter 2 Emoji Lexicon	16
Chapter 2 & Comment Threads	18
Chapter 2 Reflection & Discussion	22
Chapter 3	25
Chapter Breakdown	25
Chapter 3 Emoji Lexicon	26
Chapter 3 & Comment Threads	28
Chapter 3 Reflection & Discussion	33
Chapter 4	37

Chapter Breakdown	37
Chapter 4 Emoji Lexicon	38
Chapter 4 & Comment Threads	40
Chapter 4 Reflection & Discussion	46
Philippians in Short	**50**
Pictorial Character Directory	**51**
Endnotes	**60**
Author Bio	**61**
What's Next for LBB?	**62**

Philippians Retweeted

Foreword

What Is Little Bird Bible?
Every day billions and billions of text messages and social media posts containing emojis are sent expressing the thoughts and feelings of people across the world in short, succinct ways, but thus far, this modern and global form of communication remains independent from the message of Holy Scripture, which we believe is also meant for all people. Thus, the idea of translating a new condensed paraphrase of the Bible using emojis and formatted within the parameters of social media came to be, and the Little Bird Bible was hatched with the mission **to simplify and enhance the Bible reading experience for 21-Century audiences.** The Spirit of God descending from heaven like a dove, as described in John 1:32, is the image and metaphor we use in our books in the hopes that your mind, imagination, and faith will similarly be inspired from on high.

What Makes The Little Bird Bible Different?

1. Illustrative language
Instead of creating a *literal equivalent translation* of the Bible, which strives to accurately translate the prose, syntax, and words of Scripture from their original languages, The Little Bird Bible is a new type of *dynamic equivalent translation*. It seeks to capture the thoughts and feelings 🥰 😖 😢 😬 of the original authors with the pictorial language of emojis and stickers. Thus, this Bible is not a replacement for traditional translations; it is a supplement for the devoted and the curious when reading their own preferred Bible translation.

What is more, even though emojis are used universally around the world through a specific, ever-expanding font called Unicode

(Currently version 13), there is disagreement about what some emojis mean. There are also many words and ideas for which no singular emoji currently exists, so The Little Bird Bible often combines several emojis to create an idea or concept. To help define and reveal the meaning of these unique emoji combinations, we also use background colors and an emoji lexicon to assist the reader.

Background Colors. The emojis used in a sequence are set on a unifying background-color block to help you interpret their compound meaning:
Tan = General,
Purple = Holy,
Black = Dark,
Red = Sinful

Chapter Lexicons. At the start of each chapter, a reference guide lays out in sequential order the key emojis and unique emoji combination as they are used for the first time in that chapter alongside their intended definitions. Emojis used in their literal or common sense are not included.

2. Perpetuating Dialogue

The Bible is often treated as a static, historic, closed, divine offering, instead of as a progressive and expanding dialogue of God's revelation to the world, so we are hopeful that every edition of the Little Bird Bible gives you, the reader, an opportunity to engage, debate, and discuss the text as well. To help facilitate this dynamic, this *Retweeted Version* of the book adds a number of comment threads indented throughout the main text. These comments are voiced by a theologically diverse cast of famous, historic, and sometimes imagined characters across time; we hope their debate and discussion of the original text from their unique faith perspectives will help you, the reader, learn about many key people in our faith history and broaden our collective theological understanding.

We hope you will continue the conversation online with your own understanding and interpretation of the text, so within each chapter, the Little Bird Bible provides a series of hashtag prompts (i.e. **#newleaf, #divinepatience**) to post on your favorite social media platforms.

3. Emotive Icons and Stickers

Where many contemporary Bible translations employ the use of religious art and icons, the Little Bird Bible takes this to the next level by introducing inline iconography; every passage of scripture is written alongside the colorful image of the individual that is speaking, writing, or quoting it. This unique inline iconography helps identify and clarify what is being said while underscoring the emotion of the text; the face of each icon changes to reflect their mood from passage to passage in addition to their age as time passes. The usage of these simple icons also creates a unifying stylized depiction of Biblical people that spans both Old and New Testaments with the intent of bringing greater harmony between them. The same stylistic approach is used for other non-Biblical characters that take part in the retweeted side conversations. To help familiarize the reader with the cast of characters, at the back of each *Retweeted Version*, you will find a special Pictorial Character Directory containing a brief biography of each person. In addition, the color of the border surrounding each character's icon, is designed to help the reader instantly and visually classify what each character's primary category is.

There are eight character categories and eight matching border colors:

1. Royal Blue: Old Testament people
2. Aqua Blue: New Testament people

3. Red: Philosophers & Theologians
4. Green: Inventors & Scientists
5. Grey: Antagonists & Critics
6. Yellow: Musicians & Artists
7. Purple: Spiritual Beings
8. Brown: Leaders & Experts

A white star indicates the character reflects a generic viewpoint but does not embody an actual person.

E-Reader Sticker Bonus

THANK YOU FOR CHOOSING THIS PRINT VERSION OF THIS LITTLE BIRD BIBLE BOOK. MANY OF OUR ICONS ARE ORIGINALLY FORMATTED AS DIGITAL STICKERS. IF IN THE FUTURE YOU PURCHASE A DIGITAL VERSION OF ANY OF OUR BOOKS, AND IF YOUR E-READER SUPPORTS GIF FILES, YOU WILL SEE THEM COME TO LIFE. THESE ANIMATED STICKERS ADD AN EXTRA LAYER OF EMOTION BEHIND THE TEXT AND AN ADDED ELEMENT OF FUN WHEN READING THE BIBLE THAT TRADITIONAL PRINT FORMATS CANNOT EXPRESS.

4. Living Footnotes

Where many Bible translations use tiny numeric footnotes to further elaborate on textual variations or historical context, the Little Bird Bible uses the side conversation dialogues to do the same thing in a more dynamic way. The dialogues provide concordance references to other Biblical passages, identify thematic and scriptural parallels, expand the historical context, and reinforce the theological value of your Bible reading experience.

Try Little Bird Bible Abridged

It is possible that you may find the side conversations and living footnotes distracting and that they keep you from enjoying this unique emoji translation of the Bible. If that is so, then please discover the *Abridged Versions* of many, but not all, Little Bird Bible books. The *Abridged Versions* use the same dynamic equivalent emoji translation of the Bible in a straight forward uninterrupted format, yet they also retain the relevant emotive icons of the New and Old Testament figures to more clearly identify who is speaking in the text. What you get is an even shorter, modern, sleek Bible translation that is more concise and focused.

Other Key Features

Every Little Bird Bible book employs a number of additional features that we you hope you will enjoy, such as
In-line Pronunciation Guides with difficult names, **Chapter Breakdowns** of what lies ahead, **140-Character Count Chapter Summaries** of what you just read, **Discussion & Reflection Questions** to connect with the text, and **Gender-Inclusive Language** for all people.

Thank you for choosing this Little Bird Bible book. I hope this and future LBB books will serve to kindle your imagination, challenge your own interpretation of Scripture, and provoke or establish a devotional life that connects you in a meaningful way to God.

To Him Be the Glory 🕊️🎼🙏!

J.B.C.

The Backstory of Philippians

The Author
The Apostle Paul wrote the original letter to the church in Philippi (fil-Lip-pie) along with 12 other letters that make up 13 books of  the New Testament. Paul originally was one of the early church's fiercest persecutors (**Acts 7:58-8:3**) before his conversion (**Acts 9:1-31)**, after which he became a missionary planting and encouraging churches through his travels and letters. Yet in spite of what he accomplished for the faith, he never seemed to grow out of the conviction that he was one of the worst sinners to have lived (**1 Timothy 1:16**) While he writes this letter to the Church of Philippi, he is in prison (probably in Rome) and is awaiting his trial before Caesar. His life hangs in the balance, his suffering is real, and yet he maintains a positive outlook on life as he encourages the church to find unity and stand firm in their faith.

The Book
Of all his letters, this book is the most personal and the most joyous. From start to finish joy fills each page, as does the centrality of Christ. Paul founded the church in Philippi on his second missionary journey from **Acts 16** around 50AD; this letter was written probably a decade later and is one of the earliest letters written by Paul. <u>Philippians is about enduring chains for eternal gains.</u>

The Audience
The church of Philippi was one of the first churches founded in Europe, but it could also be the first one, too. The people to whom Paul is writing are largely a Gentile audience not familiar with the Jewish roots of the Christian movement but also susceptible to the

variant teachings of those who were. The people of Philippi were very patriotic for their city was a distinguished military colony loyal to Caesar Augustus (Octavian), who gave the citizens special rights to govern themselves independently, to receive major tax breaks, and to be treated as if they actually lived in Italy.

Key Places

The city of Philippi was an important trade city near the Adriatic Sea and the main highway that connected Asia to the West. The city was an old Phoenician mining town that was conquered and named after Philip of Trace, the father of Alexander the Great. Philippi was a key battle sight between the forces of Octavian and Brutus in 42 BC when the Roman republic ended. Along the main road to Rome, Philippi was easy to reach by travel and by mailing letters like the one that created this book of the Bible.

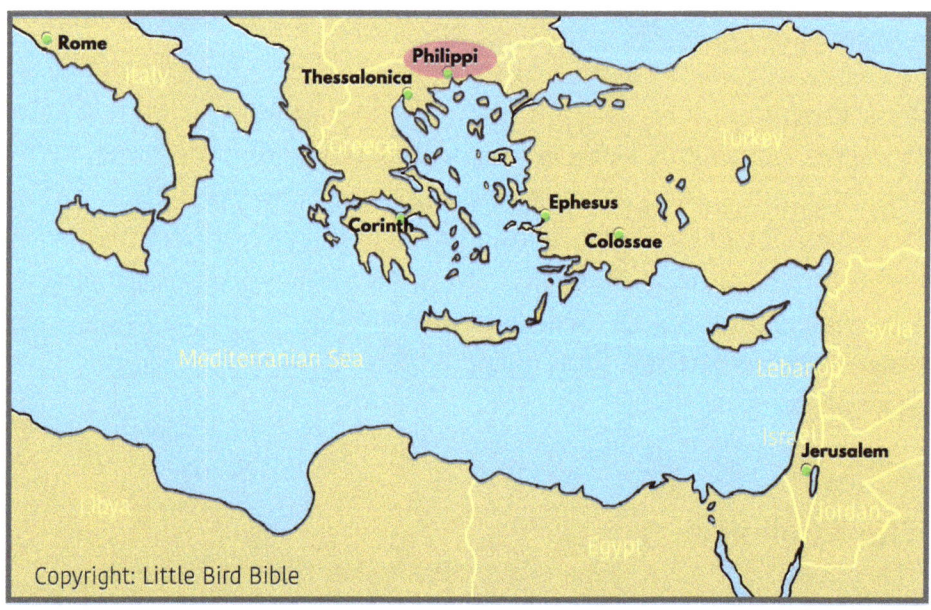

Chapter 1
Chapter Breakdown

Verses 1:1-11
Paul addresses the church in Philippi and its leaders; he shares his hopes and prayers for them and touches on all major themes of the letter.

Verses 1:12-18
Paul tells about his imprisonment and how his friends and adversaries have responded.

Verses 1:19-26
Paul shares his inner conflict, but resolves to rejoice in his suffering and to remain as their friend and advocate.

Verses 1:27-30
Paul urges the people to remain faithful in spite of their suffering and to trust in Christ just as he has.

Chapter 1 Emoji Lexicon
The sequential usage & definitions of non-literal emoji concepts

Philippians 1:1-11
✝️ =Christ
⏳🕰⌚ =Time
🤔💭 =Think/Consider
🙏 =Pray, Prayer
👍📰 =Good News/Gospel
🏁 =Finish
👍 =Good
🚧 =Work
❤️ =Heart
💗 =Love
↗️📈 =Increase
🎓🧠 =Knowledge, Smart
😇 =Holy, Pure
🍏🍒🍇 =Fruit
😇🔥 =Holy Fire

Philippians 1:12-18
🏰💂 =Palace guard
👬↔️ =Brothers
📢 =Preach
💪 =Strength
👎 =Bad
🤼📣 =Fighting, Strife

Philippians 1:19-26
🎉🤗🎺 =Rejoice
😇🕊💧 =Holy Spirit
🐛➡️🦋 =Transform
🎖 =Courage
💀 =Death
☠️ =Die, Dying
📈 =Gain
✖️2️⃣➕👍 =Better
🤔⚖️ =Choice
🍾⛲ =Overflow

Philippians 1:27-30

  =Focus

 =Travel

 =Stand Firm

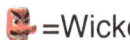=Wicked

⚠️ =Warning

=Destruction

=Salvation

 =Stand

🔗=(Together, Togetherness)

The Book of Philippians
Chapter 1 & Comment Threads

Philippians 1:1-8

Paul @WorstSinnerEver

To the Church🏛 of Philippi & its leaders: 👋 this is Paul & Timothy, both followers of Christ✝; grace & ☮ from our Lord. I thank God each time ⏳🕰⌚ that I think🤔💭 of you!

When I 🙏 for all of you, I feel great 😄 because of your partnership in the Good News👍📖. God will finish🏁 the 👍 work🚧 He began in you.

You are all in my ❤, whether in ⛓s or advancing the Gospel👍📖. We share God's grace, & God can tell you how I miss you😢 with the ❤ of Jesus ✝.

Prof. Largo @GreekScholarSupreme
The translation of "splanchnon" in Greek actually means guts, not heart. The center of all emotion rests in your guts according to the Greeks. We talk about gut feelings, ourselves.

Mr. Emoji @EmojiGuru
But there are no "gut" emojis, at least not yet; the translation is good. Today, we connect our emotions with our heart anyway; Good question, though, which do you trust more, your heart or your guts?

What do you think? Post about it:
#HeartOrGuts

Login: *Facebook*; *Instagram*; *Twitter*

Philippians 1:9-19

Paul @WorstSinnerEver

This is my 🙏 for you: that your love 💗 may increase 🔼 📈 in depth & knowledge 🎓 🧠 that you may be holy 😇 & blameless filled with the 🍏 🍒 🍇 of God's 😇 🔥 found in ✝️ until the end of time!

Don't be 😖, 😢, or 😬 for me, everyone including the palace guard 🏰 💂 know I am in ⛓s for ✝️; this is 👍 for the Gospel 👍 🗞 as our fellow brothers 👬 🔁 preach 📢 the faith with more strength 💪 & without 😬.

Now, some consider 🤔 💭 me & preach 📢 ✝️ out of love 💗 & 👍 will, but others preach 📢 out of 👎 motives 😒 🤑 😠 causing strife 🤼 🥩. But what does it matter 🤷 ⁉️ ✝️ is preached 📢, so I'm 🙂!

I will rejoice 🎉 👻 🍾, for I know through your 🙏s & the Holy Spirit 😇 👼's power, my suffering will transform 🐛 ➡️ 🦋 into my deliverance.

 **Job** @God'sFavorite
I said the same thing! **Job 13:16**

Philippians 1:20-23

 **Paul** @WorstSinnerEver
I just hope I have enough strength 💪 & courage 🎖
to keep ✝️ 🥇 st in my life or in my death 💀.
For me, to live is ✝️ and to die 💀 is gain 📈‼️

If I keep living, then my work 🚧 will bear much 🍏🍒🍇, which is 👍, but if I die 💀, then I will be with ✝️, which is better ✖️ 2️⃣ ➕ 👍.

 **Prof. Winglethrush** @LiteratureIsLife
Does that read "double plus good"? The King James Version of the Bible was the greatest achievements of our language; you've reduced it to Orwellian syntax!

 **Jarrod** @LittleBirdBible
But there still is the KJV; I am not replacing it. I contend using emoji's in the text may stimulate language & creativity in the brain.

 **William Tyndale** @FirstOfficialEnglishBible
People did not like my translation of the Bible either. I was betrayed, imprisoned for 450 days, accused of heresy, executed by strangling, and then burned at the stake. You can't please everyone. Relax.

Philippians 1:24-26

Paul @WorstSinnerEver

That is a hard choice 🤔⚖️. To be with ✝️ is better, but for your sake, I will live & work 🚧 so that the faith will grow & the 🤗 of ✝️ will overflow 🍾🥂.

Shakespeare *@TheGreatestBardEver*
"To Be or Not to Be, that is the question." I totally get you, Paul.

Dr. King *@IHaveADream*
"Every man must decide if he will walk in the light of creative altruism or the darkness of destructive selfishness."[1]

Dietrich Bonhoeffer *@SaveTheChurch*
"We must learn to regard people less in the light of what they do or omit to do, and more in the light of what they suffer."[2]

Paul *@WorstSinnerEver*
Dr. King, Dietrich—I am glad I am in the good company of souls who have suffering in prison unjustly.

Philippians 1:27-30

Paul @WorstSinnerEver

So don't worry 😨 about me, rather focus 👁️🔬 on living a life worthy of the Gospel 👍💵 of ✝️, so if I can't travel 👣👜 to see you, I will know you stand firm 👬💪⚓ as 1️⃣ in faith.

Do not 😱 about the wicked 👹 who oppose you. Don't be 🤐. Your faith is a warning ⚠️ to them of their destruction 👎🔥☠️🗑️ & a sign of your salvation 👍😇🔒🏆.

Remember ☝️ : Faith is a gift 🎁, & so is suffering. So, stand firm 👬💪⚓ together as I stand 👬 with you, & we'll make it through together 🔗

C.S. Lewis @ForNarnia
*"God whispers to us in our pleasures, speaks in our conscious, but shouts in our pain. It is his megaphone to rouse a deaf world."*³

Job *@God'sFavorite*
I lost everything. My wealth, my land, my health, and my children. Is suffering really a gift?

What do you think? Post about it:
#GiftOfSuffering

Login: *Facebook*; *Instagram*; *Twitter*

Chapter 1: Condensed

👋🏫, I 😢 you in my ❤️. I'm in ⛓️ for ✝️, but in life or in 💀, God will 🐛➡️🦋 this into 👍; be 🤗 & don't 😱 about the 👹, but 👬💪⚓ & 👁️🔬 on

Chapter 1 Reflection & Discussion

Whether you are reading as an individual or studying as a group, take some time to explore what is going on in the text and within yourself:

1. Who are the people in your life that you thank God for whenever you remember them? *(Verse 1:3)*

   _____
   _____
   _____

2. We are all works in progress, and God is not done with us yet. What good works has God begun in you that may need more time, effort, and patience to develop and perfect? *(Verse 1:6)*

   _____
   _____
   _____
   _____
   _____

3. When has the struggle or oppression you have seen others endure pressed you on to work or fight harder for a cause? *(Verse 1:14)*

   _____
   _____
   _____
   _____
   _____
   _____

4. Though he is tempted to give up, Paul determines he will stay the course for the sake of the community. When is a time that your commitment to others kept you from giving up? *(Verse 1:25)*

_____
_____
_____
_____
_____

5. "Standing Firm" (*Greek: stēkō*) is a common command Paul uses with many of the other New Testament Churches (**1 Corinthians 16:13, Galatians 5:1, 1 Thessalonians 3:8, 2 Thessalonians 2:15**) It literally means to maintain or hold the line. Where in your life is there a place you are tempted to give in, but need to stand firm? *(Verse 1:27)*

_____
_____
_____
_____

6. Paul shares that in matters of living out your faith Both suffering and belief are "graciously given" (*Greek: charizomai*). Do you think suffering is a gift? *(Verse 1:29)*

_____
_____
_____
_____
_____

Other thoughts, musings, and doodles:

_____
_____
_____
_____
_____

<u>Say a prayer:</u>
*for the names of the people you wrote down.
*for those who suffer and those in prison.

Chapter 2
Chapter Breakdown

Verses 2:1-5
Paul challenges the church to exemplify humility and unity.

Verses 2:6-11
Paul shares a hymn that shows Christ to be the perfect example of humility and obedience to God as a model to follow.

Verses 2:12-18
Paul impresses the need to meet and rise above life's challenges in order to live more faithfully.

Verses 2:19-30
Paul promises to send Timothy, to encourage and teach their congregation, and he tells of how Epaphroditus, their messenger, grew deathly ill but is returning now that God healed him.

Chapter 2 Emoji Lexicon

The sequential usage & definitions of non-literal emoji concepts

Philippians 2:1-5

💗 =Love

🙌 =Bless/Blessing

😌 =Serenity, Contentment

💥 =Power

🔗 =(Together, Togetherness)

✝️ =Christ

🤔💭 =Consider

Philippians 2:6-11

👱 =Man

📉 =(Less, Reduced)

👤 =Image

🌤🌌 =Heaven

🔥🕳☠️ =Hell

Philippians 2:12-18

💗🤝👬 =Friends

🚧🛠 =Diligently Work

👍😇🔒🏆 =Salvation

👍 =Good

💬👎😖 =Complaining

💬👎😠 =Arguing

😇 =Holy, Pure

🚸👦👧 =Children

😈 =Wicked

🚫🗑❓🔄 =Lost

🌌 =The heavens

🎙🏅 =Boast

⏳🔚 =End of time

👷🛠 =Labor(s)

💀 =Die, Dying

💁 =(Diminish)

🔙👀 =See, Look

🎉🤗🍾:🥂 =Rejoice

Philippians 2:19-30

=Send

=Soon

=Wait

=Son

=Watches

=Return

=Honor

=Good News/Gospel

The Book of Philippians
Chapter 2 & Comment Threads

Philippians 2:1-13

Paul @WorstSinnerEver
So if you have any 💗, 🤗, 🙏, 😌, 💥, 😃, or 🔗 with Christ ✝️, then make my 🤗 complete by having the same 💗, 🤗, 🙏, 😌, 💥, 😃, & 🔗 with each other.

Stop 🛑 putting yourself 🥇 st @ the expense of others, rather be humble 🙇‍♀️🙇‍♂️, & consider 🤔💭 others better than yourself; strive to be like ✝️.

"✝️ was = to God, & yet reduced 📉 himself to be a man 👱 like us in God's image 👤.
✝️ was humble 🙇, ✝️ obeyed, ✝️ died, & ✝️ was exalted 🙌.

So @ the name of Jesus, everything on 🌎, in Heaven ⛅🌌, or in Hell 🔥🕳️☠️, should bow 🙇 & every 👅 confess that Jesus ✝️ is Lord ❗"

Thus, dear friends 💗🤝👬, in my absence, continue together 🔗 to obey & diligently work 🚧🛠️ out your salvation 👍😌🔒🏆 with 😬 & 😳; for it is God who 🚧🛠️s within you to fulfill his 👍 purpose.

Stacy *@TheWhyGirl*
That doesn't make sense, why should I have to work out my salvation with fear and trembling? Isn't my salvation secure, cause I believe in Jesus?

Prof. Largo *@GreekScholarSupreme*
"Work out your salvation" in Greek is plural; the Church should do this together in Paul's absence; this is not commanding individual quests for piety.

Thomas Aquinas *@MedievalChurchDoctor*
"Those who fear while doing anything, are more apt to fail...The Apostle says 'With fear and trembling' work out your salvation: and he would not say this if fear were a hindrance to a good work. Therefore fear does not hinder a good action."[4]

St. Augustine *@HippoChurchDoctor*
"'It is God who worketh in you;' therefore 'with fear and trembling,' make a valley, receive the rain. Low grounds are filled, high grounds are dried up. Grace is rain… Fear that thou mayest be filled; be not high-minded (proud), lest thou be dried up."[5]

Angelica *@WorshipLeadingLife*
Hallelujah, Todd Agnew's song, "Grace Like Rain" has a whole new meaning! Is there or should there be fear in salvation, though?

What do you think? Post about it:
#FearInSlavation

Login: *Facebook*; *Instagram*; *Twitter*

Philippians 2:14-24

Paul @WorstSinnerEver
Do everything w/o complaining 💬 👎 😞 or arguing 💬 👎 😡, so you can become holy 😇 children 🚸 👦 👧 of God in a wicked 👿 & lost 🚫 🗺️ ❓ 🔁 generation, where you shine like ✨ ✨ ✨ in the heavens 🌌 as you keep the faith.

Moses @TheLawBeWithYou
Tell me about it! The generation I ministered to was also warped and corrupt, but what can you do? **Deuteronomy 32:5.**

Then I will boast 🎤 🏅 @ the end of time ⏳ 🔚 that I didn't labor 👷 🛠️ in vain. Even if I die 💀 & lose it all 💅 for building up the faith I see 🔙 👀 in you, I will rejoice 🎉 🤗 🍾, so 🎉 🤗 🍾 w/ me 👯 !

Isaiah @MajorOT&NTprophet
"I have labored in vain for nothing; I gave my strength to leverage nothing. But what I earn for my work is up to God; He will pay me rightly what is due." **Isaiah 49:4.**

I hope to send 🔼 Timothy to you 🔜 while I wait ⌚ ⏳ for things to resolve here. Timothy is like a son 👦 🔽 to me, who labors 👷 🛠️ with me & watches ⌚ out for you.

Philippians 2:25-30

Paul @WorstSinnerEver

I will send 📤 back 🔙 Epaphroditus *(eh-paff-Rho-dee-toss)* to you with this ✉️. He has been a huge help! He is the 💣; he was 🤢 & almost died 💀, but don't worry 😰; he is better 😀 & God is 👍.

> ***Epaphroditus** @CourierForChrist*
> *Thanks, Paul. Can you write me a letter that will be read 1000s of years later across the world & celebrated as sound faith doctrine, too?*

> ***Paul** @WorstSinnerEver*
> *What? Why would anyone want to read my letters to any of you? That's just silly. Christ will probably come back before then anyhow...*

Please welcome him 🏠 in the Lord with great 🤗, and honor ⚜️🎉🏅 men like him, for he almost 💀 d for the sake of the Good News 👍📜 to help in ways you could not.

Chapter 2: Condensed

unified in ✝️ in 💗, 🤗, 🙌, 😌, 💥, 😃, & 🔗; don't 💬👎😔 or 💬👎😠, but shine like ✨ & 🚧🛠 out your 👍😇🔒🏆. Jesus ✝️ is Lord; let 🌍, 🌤🌌, & 🔥🕳💀🙇 before him.

Chapter 2 Reflection & Discussion

Whether you are reading as an individual or studying as a group, take some time to explore what is going on in the text and within yourself:

1. Why is considering others better than ourselves such a challenging activity for most people to do? *(Verse 2:3)*

   _____

   _____

   _____

2. As part of this chapter, Paul includes a poem about Jesus that many scholarships think was a common hymn of the early church. If you were given the choice to include a hymn or praise song as part of the Bible, what song would you choose? *(Verses 2:6-11)*

   _____

   _____

   _____

   _____

3. Many believers try to work out their salvation privately and individually not collectively and communally. What is the greatest blessing with each approach? *(Verse 2:12)*

   _____

   _____

   _____

   _____

   _____

4. Are fear and salvation connected? Why/Why not? *(Verse 2:12)*

_____
_____
_____
_____

5. Stars were very important to ancient sea-faring peoples, for they helped them navigate their way on the dark ocean. What people are shining stars in your life that guide your faith? *(Verse 2:15)*

_____
_____
_____

6. Pouring yourself, your time, resources, and energy to build up someone else up can by very trying, costly, and rewarding. Who are people you have intentionally invested in that you celebrate? *(Verse 2:17)*

_____
_____
_____

7. Both Timothy and Epaphroditus were indispensable assistants to the success of Paul's ministry. What unsaid words of encouragement do you need to share with your right hand people? *(Verses 2:22;29)*

_____
_____
_____
_____

Other thoughts, musings, and doodles:

_____
_____
_____
_____
_____
_____

<u>Say a prayer:</u>
*for the names of the people you wrote down.
*for your salvation & those who fear they lack it.

Chapter 3
Chapter Breakdown

Verses 3:1-3
Paul warns the church to be on guard against a sect of believers who say circumcision is required for salvation and put their faith in their deeds.

Verses 3:4-9
Paul shares what he has lost or given up in order to follow Christ, yet how that sacrifice pales in comparison to what he has learned and gained.

Verses 3:10-14
Paul identifies the hope in becoming more and more like Christ, even in suffering, which becomes the goal of the faithful and the pattern by which we should live.

Verses 3:15-21
Paul reminds the church that ultimately their identity is not of this world but in Heaven and to turn from any path that leads away from that.

Chapter 3 Emoji Lexicon
The sequential usage & definitions of non-literal emoji concepts

Philippians 3:1-3

👨‍👩‍👧↔️=Brothers

🎉😊🍾=Rejoice

👑🔼=Lord

🔁=Repeat, Again

🔑=Of Key Importance

😠🐕=Vicious Dogs

🚧=Work

👎😾=Evil

📢=Preach

✂️🚹😫=Circumcision

✝️=Christ

🎼👼🙏🕯️=Worship

👍=Good

🙌=Bless/Blessing

❤️=Heart

🗡️📌📍=The Point

Philippians 3:4-9

🇮🇱=Israel

🚩=(People Group)

✡️=Jew

👨‍🏫✡️⚖️=Teacher of the Law

🏅💰😎🎓={Symbols of Material Success}

📈💰=Profit, Gain

📉🗑️=Loss

💩=Rubbish

Philippians 3:10-14

👍😇=Righteous

📖✡️⚖️=The Law

💥=Power

💀🔃😊🦋=Resurrection

😫👎😪=Suffering

💀=Death

🙏=Pray, Prayer

⏱️=(Countdown)

🛣️=Way, Path

🏗️⏳=(Progress)

👇⌨️=Press

Philippians 3:15-21

=Forget

=See, Look

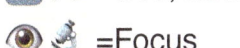=Focus

=Goal

🎉🏆💰 =Prize

📞=Calls

⛅🌌=Heaven

⌛🕰⌚ =Time

🐇🔄🎩=Reveal

🏁=Finish

🚴🚴🚴🚴=Race

🤼👎👹=Enemies

💗=Love

ℹ️=Revere

🥓💰...🎮📚=(Objects of Devotion)

👎🔥☠️🗑=Destruction

⏱⏳=Wait

🔄=Return

🐛➡️🦋=Transform

👍➕=Great

🤔💭💥=Imagine

27

The Book of Philippians
Chapter 3 & Comment Threads

Philippians 3:1-2

Paul @WorstSinnerEver
Finally, brothers 👨‍👩‍👧‍👦 🔄, rejoice 🎉 🥰 🍾 in the Lord 👑 🔺! Let me repeat 🔁 this; it is 🔑: Beware ⚠️ of those vicious dogs 😠 🐕, who work 🚧 evil 👎 😈 & preach 📢 that circumcision ✂️ 🔼 😫 is the only way to be saved 🙇.

> **Amal** @JudiazersForJesus
> Wild dogs? Paul, you are so obtuse. Moses gave us the Law & circumcision is a required part of the covenant. You are leading people astray!

>
> **Paul** @WorstSinnerEver
> Circumcision is not a prerequisite to salvation. Works, even pious self-abasing ones, will not get you one inch closer to Heaven—only faith!

Philippians 3:3

Paul @WorstSinnerEver
Rather, living our faith in ✝️ through worship 🎼 🙇 🙏 🕯️ & 👍 works 🚧 is the outward sign of God's blessing 🙌: In our ❤️s, we are the True Circumcision ✂️ 🔼 😫; they missed the point 🗡️ 📌 🎈! 😉

Moses @TheLawBeWithYou
I actually agree with Paul here, having said something very similar myself!
Deuteronomy 10:16, 30:6

Philippians 3:4-8

Paul @WorstSinnerEver

Now you've all read my file 📄: Born of Israel 🇮🇱 to an elite tribe 🚩, circumcised ✂️⬆️😫 on Day 8️⃣, a Jew ✡️ of ✡️s, & a Teacher of the Law 👨‍⚖️✡️⚖️. I was 🥇💰😎🎓 — ALL THAT + a side of 🍟.

But, ALL THAT was to my profit 📈💰, I now count as loss 📉🗑; in fact 👆, everything is a loss 📉🗑 compared to the even greater profit 📈💰 of knowing ✝️;
ALL ELSE is 💩‼️

Hellen @OffendedLayPerson
I am offended by your usage of poo in the Bible! God's Word—which I use VERY loosely here—should have dignity and class.

Prof. Largo @GreekScholarSupreme
Actually, the original Greek text says "poo" in an explicit sort of a way. So, "poo" doesn't go far enough to capture the sentiment; if there wasn't an emoji, it should read $#!%.

Jarrod *@LittleBirdBible*
I'm just trying to be faithful to the text. Do you think poo belongs in the Bible?

What do you think? Post about it:
#PooInBible

Login: Facebook; Instagram; Twitter

Philippians 3:9-12

Paul @WorstSinnerEver

So understand, righteousness 👍😇 does not come from The Law 📖✡️⚖️ or our own 🥇💰😎🎓+🍟; it comes from faith in ✝️ alone.

I want to know ✝️, the power 💥 of his resurrection 💀🎶😃🦋, & the fellowship of his suffering 😣👎😪, so I can become like him in his death 💀, & I 🙏 I discover a resurrection 💀🎶😃🦋 of my own.

I'm not there yet ⏱, but I am on the way 🛣. We are all works 🚧 in progress 🏗⏳. ✝️ saw something in me, so I will press 👇⌨️ on & not let him ⬇️.

    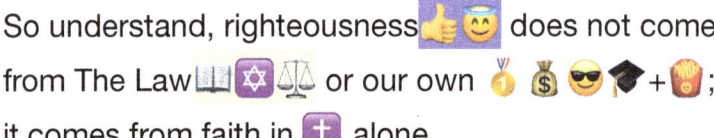 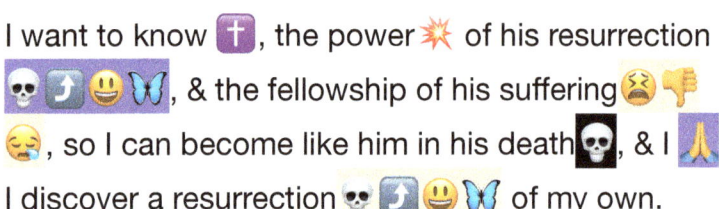

John Wesley *@FoundingMethodism*
I call this process of sanctification, "Moving onto perfection."

Philippians 3:13-21

Paul @WorstSinnerEver

So, forget ❌🤔🔙 what lies behind, only look⬅️👀 ahead, focus👁️🔬 on the goal🥅 to win the prize 🎉🏆💰, for which God calls📞 us to Heaven⛅🌌 in ✝️ Jesus.

Time ⏳🕰️⌚ will tell, & God will reveal🤫📩🎩 this is true, so join me; follow my lead, & let's finish 🏁 this race🚴🚴🚴 together.

I am 😢 to repeat🔁, that there are many who live as enemies👊👎👿 of ✝️; they love 💗 other things & revere🔼 other false "gods": 🥖💰🏈🎬☕💻🎮📚. Their destruction👎🔥☠️🗑️ is sure 😢.

But, we live for more❗ We are citizens of Heaven ⛅🌌. We wait⏱️⏳ for ✝️ to return↩️ and transform🐛➡️🦋 the 🌍 & even our own bodies into something far greater👍✝️ than we can imagine🤭🌙💥.

Guy @RandomPhilippian
Why do you question our citizenship? Wasn't our whole town of Philippi granted the privilege of being citizens of Rome, as if we lived there, given our fierce loyalty to Caesar?

Paul *@WorstSinnerEver*
My point exactly, but Heaven offers you more than a nice tax break....

Chapter 3: Condensed

We are the True ✂️🚹😫, but 👍😇ness doesn't come from us or our own 🥇💰😎🎓+🍟, but faith in ✝️ & his 💀🎵😃🦋; So, let's 🏁 this 🚴, 🚴🚴, & ⏱️⌛ for ✝️ to ↩️.

Chapter 3 Reflection & Discussion

Whether you are reading as an individual or studying as a group, take some time to explore what is going on in the text and within yourself:

1. Paul warns the people of the church to stay away from the believers who insist that following the rules and practices of the Law of Moses, like circumcision, was a necessary part of salvation. What rules or rituals do you think need to be followed for someone to be "saved"? *(Verse 3:3)*

   _____
   _____
   _____
   _____

2. Eventually Paul figured out that all the things he used to prop himself up with in life really did not matter in comparison to what he gained in Christ. When is a time your values changed and you had to reorder the priorities of your life? *(Verse 3:7)*

   _____
   _____
   _____
   _____

3. Do you think poo belongs in the Bible, or should we use language that is more tactful and polite? *(Verse 3:8)*

   _____
   _____
   _____
   _____

4. Paul encourages the Church to not dwell on what happened in the past, but to focus the on the path ahead. Where in your life do you tend to look back more than you look forward?
(Verse 3:13)

_____

_____

_____

_____

5. What do you think it means for people to live as "enemies of Christ"? Does that look different today than back in Paul's era?
(Verse 3:18)

_____

_____

_____

_____

_____

6. As people of faith, we look forward to the day when Christ will come again and transforms this world by bringing everything into right standing with Him. What do you hope he fixes first?
(Verses 3:20-21)

_____

_____

_____

_____

_____

Other thoughts, musings, and doodles:

_____

_____

_____

_____

_____

<u>Say a prayer:</u>
*for the the transformation of the world to start now.
*for those we think live as enemies of Christ

Chapter 4
Chapter Breakdown

Verses 4:1-3
Paul's urges two women in the church to find unity and stop arguing with the help of a third party.

Verses 4:4-9
Paul encourages the church to rejoice. He urges them to focus on living faithfully and not on anything that will separate or divide them, using himself as an example.

Verses 4:10-13
Paul thanks the church for equipping him so well in their generosity, but also gently asks them to stop giving as he is no longer in want.

Verses 4:14-19
Paul thinks back on how the church in Philippi were faithful in helping him start his ministry when few others would and to know that God will also bless them for their sacrifice.

Verses 4:20-23
Paul sends a shout out to all the believers in Philippi and passes on his greetings from the people serving with him from afar as he concludes his letter.

Chapter 4 Emoji Lexicon
The sequential usage & definitions of non-literal emoji concepts

Philippians 4:1-3
👫↔️=Brother
👭↔️=Sister
💗=Love
⛅🌌=Heaven
🕴💪⚓=Stand Firm
👑🔺=Lord
💗🤝👬=Friends
💬👉👉🥊=Arguing
🔗⭕👬=Unity

Philippians 4:4-9
🎉😀🍾=Rejoice
🗣=Speak, Proclaim
🔁=Repeat, Again
✝️=Christ
🔙=Back, Return
🔜=Soon
🙏=Pray, Prayer
❤️=Heart
🎓📚=Understanding

👍, 🌹 ... 🦅, 😇={Happy, Beautiful, Good Things}
👍=Good
⬅️👀=See, Look
➡️👂=Hear

Philippians 4:10-13
📩=Send, Sent
😌=Serenity, Contentment
🎓👉=Know
🤫🔒=Secret
➕💰=Rich
❌💰=Poor
😀🍔...🍰🍴=Well Fed
😔❌🍴=Starving
🐝🍁=Believe
💪=Strength

38

Philippians 4:14-19

👣👜 =Travel

⛪=Church

👍✝ =Great

💳=Credit

🙏👍=Fragrant

🎁💰 =Offering

🐑🗡🎁=Sacrifice

🙌=Bless/Blessing

🎁✝✝=Generosity, Generous

💎🏦=Treasure

👏🥚🎉 =Praise

👨‍👦🔺🌌=Father in Heaven

Philippians 4:20-23

🤔💭⬅=Remember

🤴🇮🇹🏛 =Caesar

🙏✝=Lord Jesus

👤 =Spirit

🖖=Live long & Prosper.

The Book of Philippians
Chapter 4 & Comment Threads

Philippians 4:1-3

Paul @WorstSinnerEver
Thus, brothers 👬🔁s & sisters 👭🔁s, my joy 🤗 & my 👑, whom I 💗 & long for—As citizens of Heaven 🌤️🌌, we must stand firm 👫💪⚓ in the Lord 👑🔺, my dear friends 💗🤝👬s.

On a personal 📝, please Euodia *(you-oh-Dee-ah)*, please Syntyche *(soon-Too-kkheh)*, 🛑 arguing 💬👉➡️👯. Ladies, agree 🤝 in the Lord 👑🔺; Clement, please help them. We need unity 🔗⭕👭, not ➗ or 👺.

>
> **Euodia** @HometownPhilippiGirl
> *I will apologize only if she apologizes to me first!*
>
>
> **Clement** @LoyalYokeFellow
> *I think you are missing his point. Remember what Jesus taught us?* **(Matthew 5:23-24)** *I sure wish Lydia was here.*

Philippians 4:4-13

Paul @WorstSinnerEver
So, rejoice 🎉🤗🍾 in the Lord 👑🔺 always! I will repeat 📢🔁 this: 🎉🤗🍾❗ Be kind & gentle;

place others ahead of you 💁. Remember ☝️, ✝️ is 🔙ing 🔜! So don't be 😬 about anything.

Rather, in everything by 🙏 & with thanksgiving, ask God for whatever is on your ❤️, & know his ☮️ that soars 🦅 above all understanding 🎓 📚 will guide you.

Finally, whatever is good 👍, true ❤️, beautiful 🌸, happy 🎉, lovely 🦋, pure 👶, praiseworthy 🏅, honorable ⚜️, or majestic 🏔️ —think on such things. Whatever good 👍 things you see 🔙 👀 me do or hear ➡️ 👂 me say 🗣 —you do it, too.

I rejoice 🎉 🥰 🍾 for the 🎁s you 🛐. Thank you! Whatever 👰 life brings me, I have learned to be content 😌, since I have known 🎓 👉 how to live with a lot & also very little.

Knowing 🎓 👉 both is the secret 🤫 🔒 to being content: ⬆️ or ⬇️, ➕ 💰 or ❌ 💰,
😄 🍔 🍓 🔍 🥥 🍕 🍱 🍲 🥗 🍰 🍴 or 😔 ❌ 🍴,
I believe 🐝 🍁 that I 🥫 do ALL things,
thru ✝️ who gives me strength 💪‼️

Bernard of Clairvaux
@MitigatorOfPopes
"The trial of a Rule somewhat more strict often suffices to calm unquiet

spirits who are not content with the kind of life that they are living."

Thomas à Kempis *@ImitationOfChrist*
"Learn to do with little, and to be content with what is mean and poor; so will you be kept from grumbling, and will have peace in yourself, and favor with Almighty God."7

Karl Barth *@TheChurchDogmatics*
"'Joy' in Philippians is a defiant 'Nevertheless!' that Paul sets like a full stop against the Philippians' anxiety."8

Jarrod *@LittleBirdBible*
Paul was in prison in Philippi when the earth shook and he was miraculously broken free. Perhaps that gave him confidence in containment Acts 17

What do you think? Post about it.
#SecretOfContentment

Login: Facebook; Instagram; Twitter

Philippians 4:14-18

Paul @WorstSinnerEver

You know 🎓👆, when I first traveled 👣👜 to your region starting ⛪s, only you helped me back ⏪ then, to your great 👍➕💳. Thank you again 🔁 & 🔁 for each 🎁.

They are a fragrant 🙏👍 offering 🎁💰, an acceptable sacrifice 🐑🗡🎁, pleasing 😄 to God. Thanks to you & Epaphroditus *(eh-paff-Rho-dee-toss)*, I lack 🚫 thing. 😬 not! God will bless 🙌 you in return 🔁.

> **Moses** @TheLawBeWithYou
> *God is all about offerings with pleasing aromas:*
> **Leviticus 1:9, 1:13, 1:17, 2:2, 2:9, 2:12, 3:5, 3:16; 4:31, 6:15, 6:21, 8:21, 8:28, 17:6, 23:13, 23:18, 26:31**

Philippians 4:19-20

Paul @WorstSinnerEver

I know 🎓👆 this, for your generosity 🎁➕➕ is a blessing 🙌 that comes from the treasures 💎🏦 found in ✝ that flow from our 🎁➕➕ God! O Praise 👏🗣🎉 God, our Heavenly Father 👨‍👦‍👦🔺🌌, forever! Amen.

Timothy @ApprentisToPaul
So you are grateful, but you want them to stop giving you so much, lest they think they can buy you. So, you then suggest the real debt is paid to God? Brilliant!

Philippians 4:21-23

Paul @WorstSinnerEver

Greet 👋 🤝 all the ✝️-followers there, remember 🤔 💭 🔙 those with me, & esp. know 👨‍🎓 👉 those serving in the 🏠 of Caesar 👑 🇮🇹 🏛 say 👋. The grace of the Lord 👑 ✝️ be with your spirit 👤 🕊! 🖐 Amen.

Emperor Nero @CaesarWithAFiddle
What Christians in my house? I will find them and use them as torches to light my lavish dinner parties.

Eugene @42JediKirk
Live Long and Prosper, too, Paul!

Jesus @LivingWater&Life
"Peace I leave with you; my peace I give you; peace of mind and peace of heart; so don't be troubled or afraid."
(John 14:27)

Chapter 4: Condensed

Thank you for your 🎁➕➕, but dear 💗🤝👬s, we need 🔗⭕👯, & to learn to be 😌. So, 🎉🤗🍾 in the 👯🔺 always! 🐝🍁, & 🤔 about everything that is 👍.🖖!

Chapter 4 Reflection & Discussion

Whether you are reading as an individual or studying as a group, take some time to explore what is going on in the text and within yourself:

1. Euodia and Syntyche got into an argument of some sort that took root and threatened to split the church. What people in your faith community do you need to make amends with for the sake of the parish? *(Verse 4:2)*

   _____
   _____
   _____

2. Around what issue do you think the Church today needs more unity and less drama? *(Verse 4:2)*

   _____
   _____
   _____
   _____

3. What are noble, beautiful, positive, lovely, right and true things you can reflect on to reframe your mind when you are tired, tempted, & down? *(Verse 4:8)*

   _____
   _____
   _____
   _____

4. Paul asks the church to follow his example and lead a life that reflects the love of Jesus. Who are the spiritual leaders or mentors you would want to pattern your life after? Why them? *(Verse 4:9)*

_____
_____
_____
_____

5. Much of the marketing in the culture bank on people not being content. What do you do to find contentment in a world that always offers something new? (*Verse 4:11*)

   _____
   _____
   _____
   _____
   _____

6. When you had a fresh start at something new in life or in work, who were the people that helped you get started and teach you the ropes? (*Verse 4:15*)

   _____
   _____
   _____
   _____
   _____

7. Do you believe God is generous? (*Verse 4:19*)

   _____
   _____
   _____
   _____

Other thoughts, musings, and doodles:

_____

_____

_____

_____

_____

Say a prayer:
*for the names of the people you wrote down.
*for Peace, Unity, and Contentment.

Philippians in Short

Chapter 1: Condensed
👋🏛️, I 😢 you in my ❤️. I'm in ⛓️ for ✝️, but in life or in 💀, God will 🐛➡️🦋 this into 👍; be 😇 & don't 😱 about the 👹, but 👬💪⚓ & 👁️🔬 on the 👍🎞️.

Chapter 2: Condensed
Be unified in ✝️ in ❤️, 🤗, 🙌, 😌, 💥, 😃, & 🔗; don't 💬👎😔 or 💬👎😠, but 🌅 like ✨ & 🚧 🔧 out your 👍😇🔒🏆. Jesus ✝️ is Lord; let 🌍, 🌤️🌌, & 🔥🕳️☠️👑 before him.

Chapter 3: Condensed
We are the True ✂️✝️😫, but 👍😇ness doesn't come from us or our own 🏅💰😎🎓+🍟, but faith in ✝️ & his 💀🔀😃🦋; So, let's 🏁 this 🚴 🚴‍♂️🚴‍♀️🚴, & ⏱️⏳ for ✝️ to 🔙.

Chapter 4: Condensed
Thank you for your 🎁➕➕, but dear 💜🤝👬s, we need 🔗⭕🙌, & to learn to be 😌. So, 🎉😇🍾 in the 👑🔼 always! 🐝🍁, & 🤔 about everything that is 👍✌️!

Pictorial Character Directory
Cast of characters in alphabetical order

NOTE:
All characters real, historic, or imagined may have no knowledge or concept of the Little Bird Bible
and thus do not endorse it.

The color of the box around the picture indicates their primary category:
1. Royal Blue: Old Testament people.
2. Aqua Blue: New Testament people.
3. Red: Philosophers & Theologians.
4. Green: Inventors & Scientists.
5. Grey: Antagonists & Critics
6. Yellow: Musicians & Artists
7. Purple: Spiritual Beings
8. Brown: Leaders & Experts

A white star indicates the character reflects a generic viewpoint but does not embody an actual person.

Amal @JudiazersForJesus. Amal is the voice of opposition in the church of Philippi. He is part of a group called Judaizers, who though they believed in the divinity of Christ, also believe that adhering to the Law of Moses is necessary for salvation to be complete.

Angelica @WorshipLeadingLife. Angelica is the voice of modern contemporary worship leaders. She is full of passion, praise, and the Holy Spirit as she leads others to witness the spirit of God through music.

Bernard of Clairvaux @MitigatorOfPopes. (1090-1153AD) Bernard was a humble French abbot, who went on to reform a monastic Order, become an adviser to numerous Popes, promote the (failed) Second Crusade, and preside over the special called council to resolve the Great Schism between rival Popes in 1130. He was one of the most influential men of the 12th Century. He died at home in the Abbey.

C.S. Lewis @ForNarnia.(1898-1963AD) Clive Staples Lewis was an English professor at Oxford and a noted atheist, until his conversion to Christianity. Beyond the Chronicles of Narnia, he wrote, taught, and defended the philosophical positions of Christian teaching through numbers non-fiction books and radio broadcasts. After a year of declining health, he collapsed at home and died of renal failure.

Dietrich Bonhoeffer @SaveTheChurch. (1906-1945AD) Bonhoeffer was a German theologian, Lutheran Pastor, and founding member of the Confessing Church. During the Nazi occupation of Germany, he led the underground church teaching pastors secretly in the woods; he was arrested in the conspiracy to kill Hitler, and sent to prison where he wrote his most famous work, *Ethics*. He was executed on the gallows of Flossenbürg Concentration Camp several days before it was liberated.

Dr. King @IHaveADream. (1929-1968AD) Dr. Martin Luther King, Jr. was an American Baptist minister and an outspoken activist during the American Civil Rights Movement from 1954 until his death. His passionate voice for racial equality and practice of non-violent civil disobedience inspired the world and won him the Nobel Peace

Prize in 1964. He was assassinated by a gunman in Memphis, TN, while planning a national rally to occupy Washington, D.C.

Emperor Nero @CaesarWithAFiddle. (37-68AD) Nero was the 6th Emperor of Rome following Claudius in succession (whom he may have plotted to kill). He reigned as Caesar for 13 years. He is rumored to have played the fiddle while watching Rome burn (a fire he may have started to make room for his new palace). He is also known for using Christians as human torches to light his lavish dinner parties. He was the first Emperor to commit suicide.

Epaphroditus @CourierForChrist. *(eh-paff-Rho-dee-toss)* Epaphroditus was a messenger of the church of Philippi, who delivered gifts to Paul while he was in prison in Rome (**Philippians 4:18**) and assist him in his work (**Philippians 2:25**). He in only mentioned in this book of the Bible, and all we know of him is how he became deathly ill during his visit; Paul sends him back with his letter when he was well again.

Eugene @42JediKirk. Eugene is the Little Bird Bible's resident software engineer and data analysts. He loves Sci-Fi, computers, and tech trends in our culture. He is also fluent in Klingon.

Euodia @HometownPhilippiGirl. *(you-oh-Dee-ah) Euodia* was a female leader in the church of Philippi and possibly a deaconess. She is only mentioned once in the Bible (**Philippians 4:2**) where she is tasked to resolve her dispute with another woman in the parish since their conflict was eroding the unity of the burgeoning church.

Guy @RandomPhilippian. is the voice of the average Roman citizen living in Philippi at the time of Paul starting the church there. Christian teaching and Jewish traditions are all very new to him, so he is skeptical and sometimes defiant in reorienting his life to a culture different than what he knew growing up in the secular Roman world.

Hellen @OffendedLayPerson. Hellen is the voice of the hard-to-please long-standing members of the local church, who are not afraid to share their grievances and opinions.

Isaiah @MajorOT&NTprophet. (740-690BC) Isaiah is one of the major prophets of the Old Testament. He is attributed with writing the Book of Isaiah. He prophesied in the royal court of several Kings of Israel during the expansion of the Assyrian Empire that threatened Israel's sovereignty and future. Isaiah married a prophetess and had two sons. Thematically, Isaiah calls Israel to repent in chapters 1-39 for some 20 years before the nation of Assyrian conquers the Northing Kingdom; however, there is a transition that takes place starting in Chapter 40 onward where the emphasis shifts to God's people returning from Babylon's captivity; this suggests that perhaps 2 or 3 prophets may have shared God's message towards the end of the book. Isaiah is quoted very frequently in the New Testament, and most Christians accept the description of the Suffering Servant (Isaiah 52-53) as a prophesy about Jesus' crucifixion.

Jarrod @LittleBirdBible. Jarrod is the author and creator of the Little Bird Bible. Jarrod occasionally weighs in to clarify the intent and inspiration behind the translation as he strives to simplify and enhance the

Bible reading experience. In addition, at times Jarrod shares some of his own scriptural revelations he discovered during his study and translation. His biography is in the back of the book.

Jesus @LivingWater&Life. Jesus of Nazareth was a 1st Century Jewish rabbi; his disciples believed he was the Messiah and gave him the Greek title "Christ." His life and teachings are best preserved in the New Testament books of **Matthew, Mark, Luke,** and **John.** He was executed on a cross as an insurrectionist and enemy of Rome around 32 AD. People commonly understood that he was a teacher, healer, and prophet, but through his own words and the writings of Holy Scripture, Christians across time believe that he rose again from the dead because he is something more: the Son of God; the second person of the Trinity; the Way, the Truth, and the Life; the manifestation of God's divine love and power in human form; the savior of the world; the redeemer of humanity, and more. We hope you draw your own conclusions through your own reading and study.

Job @God'sFavorite. Job was a holy man who, because of his great righteousness, was put to the ultimate test of faith when he lost everything he possessed and nearly everyone he loved at the same time. In spite of this, he maintained his faith in the Almighty. You can read more about him in the **Book of Job** in the Old Testament.

John Wesley @FoundingMethodism. (1703-1791) Wesley was an Anglican priest who went on to be the founder of the Methodist Church. Although he had been ordained 13 years before, Wesley had a profound spiritual experience at a bible study on Aldersgate Street in London on May, 24 1738, where he felt his heart "strangely warmed." It was there where his heart took hold of the Gospel, and from age 35 to his death, he saw his life as a mission to preach salvation by faith. He became known for his passionate preaching, which he did wherever he could and often in the fields outside the city limits since he was often forbidden to preach in town. He died of natural causes at home.

Karl Barth @TheChurchDogmatics. (1886-1968) Karl Barth was a pastor and a prolific Swiss Reformed theologian. He became disenchanted with Protestant Liberal Theology and trail-blazed his own theological direction. His greatest work was the Church Dogmatics; spanning over five volumes across 9,000 pages, it is one of the longest works of systematic theology ever written; it was also never finished. Barth died quietly at home of heart failure.

Moses @TheLawBeWithYou. Moses lived around 1300 BC. He was one of the greatest prophets of the Old Testament; he led the Exodus out of Egypt and established the Law for the people of Israel. The Bible tells us he was unique and spoke to God face to face (**Exodus 33:11**). Moses led the people out of slavery in Egypt, governed them in the desert for 40 years, and brought them to the edge of the promised land, where he died—never crossing over into it himself. When he died, God himself buried him privately. His grave was never known or marked; some scholars assume this was to keep his tomb from becoming an idol (**Deuteronomy 34:5-6**).

Mr. Emoji @EmojiGuru. Mr. Emoji is the Little Bird Bible's resident expert on emoji creation and development. He is one of the world's front-running experts on emojis due to his knack for integrating technology, language, and Unicode.

Paul @WorstSinnerEver. (?-65 AD) Paul was a distinguished Jewish leader and Pharisee with a brilliant mind and incredible zeal, who started out persecuting Christians before his conversion to the faith. He then became one of their greatest missionaries and authors, credited with writing 13 of the 27 books found in the New Testament, and he still believed that he was one of the worst sinners to have lived (**1Timothy 1:15-16**). Tradition says that after standing trial, Paul was decapitated by orders of Emperor Nero.

Prof. Largo @GreekScholarSupreme. Largo is the Little Bird Bible's resident Greek scholar. Professor Largo excels at highlighting the importance of the usage and nuance of Greek words in the New Testament. He can simplify and teach concepts and syntax to students at any level.

Prof. Winglethrush @LiteratureIsLife. Winglethrush is the Little Bird Bible's resident literary scholar. She is an enthusiast of the Classics of Western Literature, and she has a keen eye for English grammar and syntax.

Shakespeare @TheGreatestBardEver. (1564?-1616 AD) William Shakespeare is considered to be one of the greatest communicators of the English language. This famous bard and champion of iambic pentameter is credited with the creation of approximately 39 plays and 154 sonnets. His works have subsequently been translated into most of the world's languages, and his works are performed more frequently than any other playwright. History surmises that he took suddenly ill and died.

Stacy @TheWhyGirl. Stacy is the voice of Generation Z. Stacy does not identify as religious, greatly distrusts authority structures, and is not satisfied with easy answers. Stacy must always get to the bottom of things. She is not afraid to ask bold or awkward questions to cultivate a deeper understanding.

St. Thomas Aquinas @MedievalChurchDoctor. (1225-1275AD) Aquinas was one of the most influential theologians of the medieval period and principal contributors to Western philosophy. As a Doctor of the Church, he strived to blend Aristotle's philosophy and Christian ethics into one paradigm. He died while giving commentary on the Song of Songs while on his way to a Council that Pope Urban IV called to try to reunite the Roman Catholic and Greek Orthodox Churches.

St. Augustine @HippoChurchDoctor. (354-430AD) Augustine was a Bishop from North Africa and Doctor of the Church who lived and wrote during the decay of the Roman world. As an ancient philosopher, his contributions greatly influenced Christian teaching and Western thought more than most other thinkers of his era. He grew ill and died during an extended siege by Germanic tribes against his home town of Hippo.

Clement @LoyalYokeFellow. In the conflict between Euodia and Syntyche, Clement is named to help assist in the resolution along with Syzygos. In Greek, syzygos means a "yokefellow"; some scholars believe Paul is using it as his proper name, while others think it is a pronoun for an unnamed church leader, others claim Paul is calling Euodia, Syntyche, and Clement all yokefellows. Eitherway, **Philippians 4:3** is the only reference to this person in the Bible.

Thomas à Kempis @ImitationOfChrist. (1380-1471AD) Thomas à Kempis was a Dutch-German priest living a monastic life copying and transcribing the Bible. He wrote a few books of his own, most notably "The Imitation of Christ," which Sir Thomas More said should be one of the books everyone should own. He grew ill and died at age 91; he became a candidate for sainthood some 200 years later; when his body was exhumed, they found claw marks on the inside of his coffin lid revealing he was accidentally buried alive.

Timothy @ApprentisToPaul. Timothy is a native of Lystra, a student of Paul, and a traveling missionary. He first appears in (**Acts 16:1-2**) and is mentioned throughout the New Testament in 10 of the 13 books written by Paul. (**Acts 17:14; 18:5; 19:22; 20:4; Rom 16:21; 1 Cor 4:17; 16:10; 2 Cor 1:1,19; Phil 1:1; 2:19; Col 1:1; 1 Thes 1:1; 3:2, 6; 2 Thes 1:1; 1 Tim 1:2, 18; 6:20; 2 Tim 1:2; & Philemon 1**) He is held in higher esteem than any other of Paul's companions. He was stoned to death after being beaten and drug through the streets at age 80 while trying to preach to an angry mob.

William Tyndale @FirstOfficialEnglishBible. (1494-1536AD) Tyndale was an English scholar and leader of the Protestant Reformation. His writings influenced Henry VIII to separate from the Roman Catholic Church. Tyndale produced a literal equivalent translation of the Bible in English directly from Hebrew and Greek in secret, as it was against the law. Then, he mass produced it using the printing press; over 3/4ths of the King James Bible uses Tyndale's translation. He was labeled a heretic; he was executed by strangling, and then burnt at the stake.

Endnotes

1. King Jr., Martin Luther Strength to Love Series, Sermon: "Three Dimensions of a Complete Life," Start Page 67, Quote Page 72, Published by Harper & Row, New York. 1963

2. Bonhoeffer, Dietrich, "Dietrich Bonhoeffer: Witness to Jesus Christ (Making of Modern Theology)" John W. De Gruchy (Ed.) Fortress Press, Minneapolis 1991 p.262

3. Lewis, C. S. (2001). The Problem of Pain (p. 91). New York: HarperOne.

4. Thomas Aquinas. (n.d.). Summa theologica. (Fathers of the English Dominican Province, Trans.). London: Burns Oates & Washbourne.

5. Augustine of Hippo. (1888). Sermons on Selected Lessons of the New Testament. In P. Schaff (Ed.), R. G. MacMullen (Trans.), Saint Augustin: Sermon on the Mount, Harmony of the Gospels, Homilies on the Gospels (Vol. 6, p. 502). New York: Christian Literature Company.

6. Bernard of Clairvaux: Ritzema, E., & Brant, R. (Eds.). (2013). 300 quotations for preachers from the Medieval church. Bellingham, WA: Lexham Press.

7. Thomas a Kempis: Ritzema, E., & Brant, R. (Eds.). (2013). 300 quotations for preachers from the Medieval church. Bellingham, WA: Lexham Press.

8. "Karl Barth." AZQuotes.com. Wind and Fly LTD, 2022. 22 August 2022.https://www.azquotes.com/quote/450892.

Author Bio

Jarrod Branson Conyers has been studying and teaching the Bible to both young people and adults for the past 24 years. His passion is innovating new ways to connect people to Holy Scripture. His Bachelor of Arts in Sociology and his Master of Arts in Christian Ministry poured the foundation of his profound interest in understanding culture, technology, exploring the nuance of words current and ancient, and sharing the Good News 👍📜. Jarrod lives in Albuquerque, NM, with his wife and children; he enjoys poetry, still life photography, and board games. You can email Jarrod directly at Jarrod@littlebirdbible.com, and you can like and follow the Little Bird Bible on Facebook, Twitter, and Instagram.

What's Next for LBB?

The Little Bird Bible LLC is currently developing the next several books of the Bible in this fun and exciting new format. The LBB plans to eventually release all 66 books of the Bible. The next book released will be the **Book of Mark**, but you can go to www.littlebirdbible.com and vote on the books you want to see expedited to the front of the line. You can also drop us a question to add to our FAQ on our website if you are curious about some aspect of the book you just read.

**If you enjoyed this book,
please spread the word about Little Bird:**

- Please take time rate the book online.
- Please recommend us on Goodreads.com.
- Please find, follow, and like us on:
  facebook.com/littlebirdbible
  or on Twitter via *Logos@LittleBirdBible*.
- Please continue any of the discussions on social media with the provided hashtag prompts.
- Please subscribe our email list on our website to get news and updates on our new releases.

Thank you for buying our book and supporting our mission to simplify and enhance the Bible reading experience for 21st Century audiences!

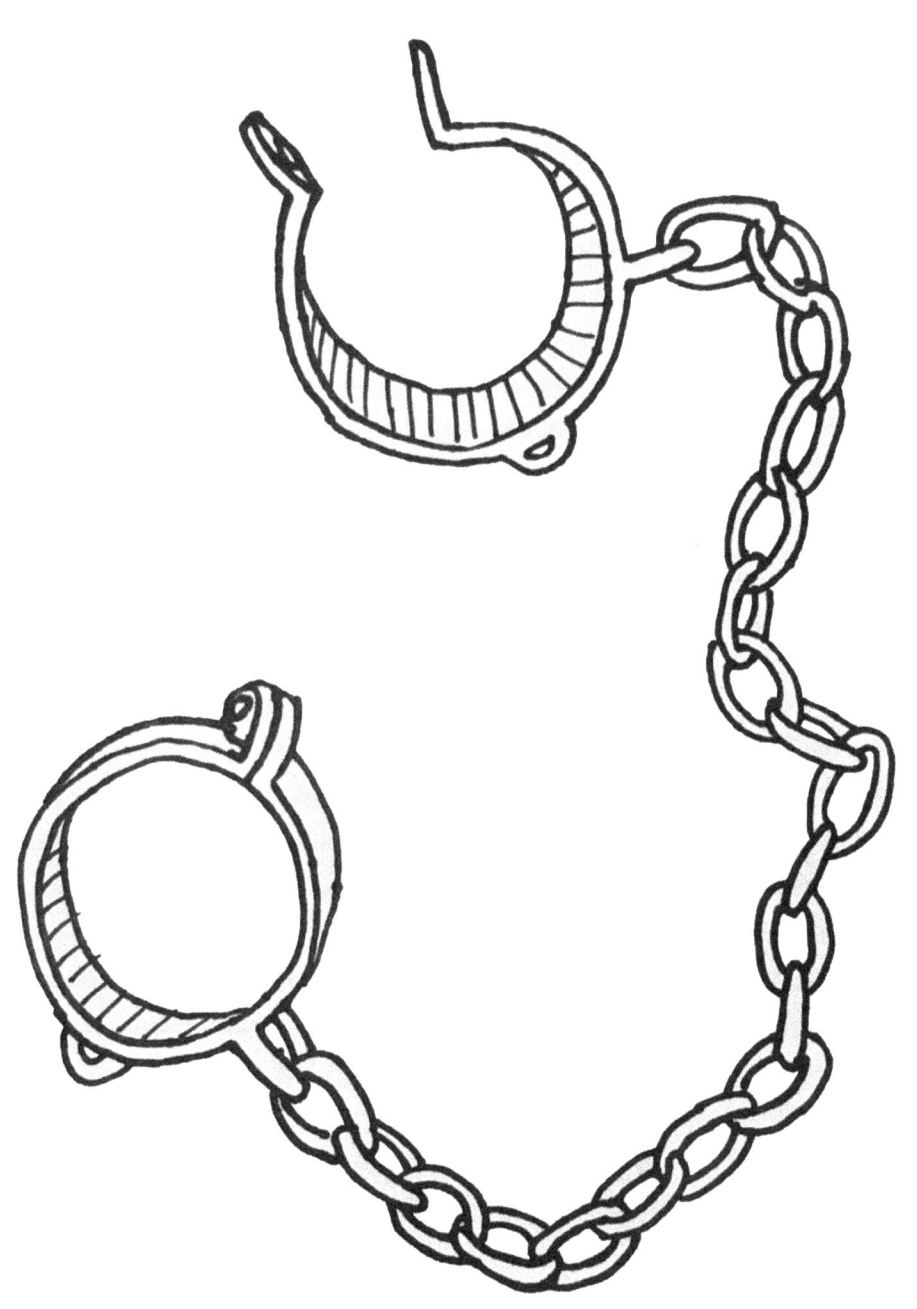

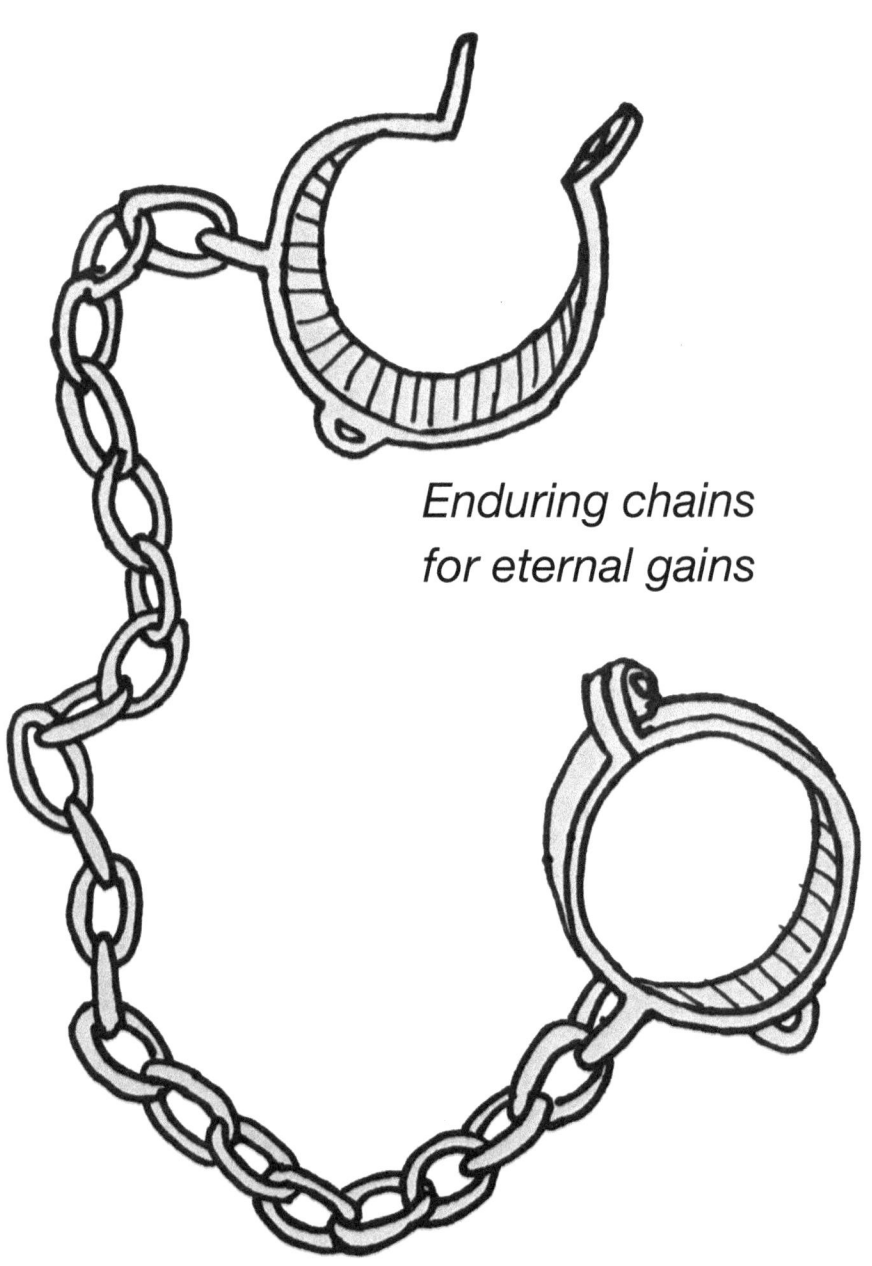

*Enduring chains
for eternal gains*

www.ingramcontent.com/pod-product-compliance
Lightning Source LLC
Chambersburg PA
CBHW061211070526
44583CB00025B/3208